POSTCARD HISTORY SERIES

Norristown

POSTCARD HISTORY SERIES

Norristown

Phillip and Sharon Welsh

ARCADIA

First printed in 2002.

Published by Arcadia Publishing,
an imprint of Tempus Publishing, Inc.
2A Cumberland Street
Charleston, SC 29401

Printed in Great Britain.

Library of Congress Catalog Card Number: 2002109309

For all general information contact Arcadia Publishing at:
Telephone 843-853-2070
Fax 843-853-0044
E-Mail sales@arcadiapublishing.com

For customer service and orders:
Toll-Free 1-888-313-2665

Visit us on the internet at http://www.arcadiapublishing.com

Main Street, Norristown, Pa.

Norristown, the county seat of government, was a vibrant center for business, commerce, industry, and transportation at the turn of the 20th century. Prosperity resulted in the expansion of the borough limits twice before 1900. Today, the Borough of Norristown is 3.69 square miles, with a population of approximately 31,000 residents. Loss of industry and retail over the last few decades left the borough less appealing to new business. Through the efforts of concerned citizens, civic leaders, and borough government, Norristown is on the road to economic recovery. Long-term revitalization projects are bringing the town back to its former glory. In 2012, Norristown will celebrate its bicentennial anniversary.

CONTENTS

BIBLIOGRAPHY

Alderfer, Gordon E. *The Montgomery County Story*. Norristown, PA: Commissioner of Montgomery County, 1951.

Bean. *History of Montgomery County*. Vol. I, II. 1884.

Daub, William Beyer. "Chapter 35: Norristown." *Montgomery County, The Second Hundred Years*. Vol. II. Norristown, PA: Montgomery County Federation of Historical Societies, 1983.

Elmwood Park Zoo. www.elmwoodparkzoo.com. Norristown, PA.

Goldstein, Sidney. *The Norristown Study*. Philadelphia: University of Pennsylvania,1961.

Heysham, Theodore. *Norristown–1812–1912*. Norristown: Norristown Herald Printers, 1913.

Historical Society of Montgomery County. *Historical Sketches*. Vol. I–V. Norristown, PA: Herald Printing and Binding.

H.W. Kriebel. *A Brief History of Montgomery County Pennsylvania*. Norristown, PA: Norristown Herald Printing and Publishing Company, 1923.

J.L. Smith. *Property Atlas of Montgomery County Pennsylvania*. Philadelphia: 1893.

Lachenmayer, J. *Norristown Hose Company Quasquicentennial 1847–1972*. Norristown, PA: Norristown Hose Company Publication Committee.

McDade, George. *Norristown, Past, Present and Future*. Norristown, PA: Norristown Herald, 1899.

McDonough, Richard A. *The history of the Norristown area (East Norriton, Norristown, and West Norriton)*. Norristown, PA: Norristown Area School District, *c.* 1980.

Montgomery Hose and Steam Fire Engine Company No. 1, Norristown, PA. *Events of a half century . . .1847–1897*. Norristown, PA: 1897.

Sesquicentennial Committee. *Sesquicentennial 1812–1912 Norristown Pennsylvania*. Norristown, PA: 1962.

The Borough of Norristown. www.norristown.org. Norristown, PA: Borough of Norristown, PA, 2000.

The Norristown Preservation Society. www.norristownpreservationsociety.com. Norristown, PA: The Norristown Preservation Society, 2001.

The Norristown Preservation Society. "Town History." www.norristown.com. Norristown, PA: webmaster Drew Salamone, 2002.

Toll, Jean Barth and Michael J. Schwager, eds. *Montgomery County, The Second Hundred Years*. Vol. I–II: Montgomery County Federation of Historical Societies, 1983.

INTRODUCTION

The Borough of Norristown is located in Montgomery County, Pennsylvania, approximately 16 miles northwest of Philadelphia, along the banks of the Schuylkill River. In 1704, William Penn Jr. received this land from his father who named the estate "Williamstadt" to honor his son. On October 7, 1704, the land was sold to Isaac Norris and William Trent. William Trent soon sold his interest to Isaac Norris, and the little village became known as "Norritingham" and "Norriton." In 1784, the boundaries of Montgomery County were formally drawn, and the town was designated the county seat of government.

In 1812, the area was incorporated as a borough and officially renamed Norristown. Norristown quickly grew into a commercial and industrial center due largely to the development of transportation systems. In 1812, a 24-mile roadway from Philadelphia to the Perkiomen Bridge passed through the borough with a 2-mile stretch along Main Street. In 1832, the Schuylkill Canal was completed, allowing local products such as coal and produce to be taken to Philadelphia and for fine goods to be sent back. Shortly after the canal system was in operation, Norristown was linked to Philadelphia by railway, allowing massive quantities of locally milled iron and marble to be transported more quickly and cheaper. Advancements in communication were made in the 1850s when local inventor and engineer Samuel Zook connected Norristown to Philadelphia via the telegraph. His invention preceded a similar device perfected by Samuel F.B. Morse.

Norristown was a major stop on the Underground Railroad, prior to the Civil War. Local abolitionists provided runaway slaves with shelter and provisions to aid them in their flight to freedom. When flight turned to fight during the American Civil War, Norristown proudly sent five of her sons to serve in the Union Army as generals. Among these men were Maj. Gen. Winfield Scott Hancock, hero of the battle of Gettysburg, and his close friend Bvt. Maj. Gen. John Hartranft, who received the congressional Medal of Honor for gallantry at the Battle of First Manassas. Maj. Gen. Winfield Scott Hancock's political aspirations after the war earned him the governorship of Pennsylvania and the presidential candidacy on the Democratic ticket in 1880. He lost to James Garfield in the election for president by only a small margin.

Norristown has been home to many other talented and prominent individuals including: Revolutionary War Gen. Andrew Porter; astronomer and instrument and clock maker David Rittenhouse; artist James John Audubon; inventor, pioneer aeronaut, and industrialist Thaddeus Sobielski Lowe; Los Angeles Dodgers manager Tommy La Sorda; New York Mets catcher Mike Piazza; actress Maria Bello; international jazz pianist Jimmy Smith; and prize-winning children's author Jerry Spinelli, just to name a few.

Norristown brings to life the town that these individuals and countless others have called home through a collection of vintage postcards from the beginning of the 20th century. As you turn the pages, you will be presented with images of the simpler time of horse-drawn carriages, beautiful estate homes, and picnics in the park. *Norristown* offers a brief glimpse of the history, character, and grandeur of Norristown. With every turn of the page, one discovers the town that was once called "the finest town in all the United States."

One
STRETCHED ALONG
THE SCHUYLKILL

View of Norristown, Pa.

Lush, abounding in resources, and stretching along a free-flowing navigable river was how the first settlers described this area more then 200 years ago. Norristown is located in Montgomery County, approximately 16 miles northwest of Philadelphia along the Schuylkill River.

Norristown was incorporated in 1812, but the town's entrepreneurial beginnings date back to the 1700s. Its proximity to Philadelphia and ideal location along a navigable river spurred the growth of industry and commerce more then a generation before the county was founded.

In 1784, the Town of Norris, as it was called then, got an economic boost when it was designated as the county seat for Montgomery County. In 1812, when the town was incorporated and renamed Norristown, various mills were in steady operation, and retail businesses started to expand into the heart of town.

Norristown, Pennsylvania

As Norristown grew economically in the 1800s, the population of this small county seat expanded. Immigrants looking for steady work in the mills and factories bought land and built homes. Over a 50-year period from 1820 to 1870, Norristown's population grew from 827 residents to 10,753.

General View of Norristown, Pa.

By the late 1800s, the town had expanded from a river-front wilderness to a thriving economic community making significant strides in industry, retail, banking, and county government. With the expansion of business and industry came the development of vital transportation corridors such as the Schuylkill Canal and Philadelphia & Reading Railroad.

The Philadelphia & Reading R. R. Bridge crossing the Schuylkill River, Norristown, Pa.

In 1848, a toll bridge was built over the Schuylkill at Ford Street for the Philadelphia & Reading Railroad. The bridge burned twice in 1883 and again in 1924. The Federal Bridge Company, the owners of the bridge, demolished it in 1939 due to continued losses.

In 1829, a wooden covered toll-bridge was constructed to span the river at DeKalb Street. The bridge was a successful investment for its stockholders, paying dividends as high as 13 percent on the stock. In 1861, the bridge was rebuilt, and in 1885, it became the property of the county and a free thoroughfare. A fire destroyed the wooden bridge in 1924, and a concrete bridge was built to take its place.

24 PHILADELPHIA AND WESTERN TROLLEY BRIDGE, NORRISTOWN, PA

The Philadelphia and Western Railway Company began service between Norristown and Sixty-ninth Street in Upper Darby in 1912. This is a partial view of the very long bridge that carried the trolley across the Schuylkill. Alongside the bridge is one of the many textile mills that lined the river-front.

The Schuylkill River has been used for fishing, swimming, and boating since the Lenni Lenape tribes roamed these shores. Some successful bankers, mill owners, and wealthy families in Norristown built impressive homes with boathouses along the river.

13

The Dam, Norristown, Pa.

Thirty-two dams were completed by 1828 for the Schuylkill Canal system. These dams were built to create long pools of water deep enough for canal boats to navigate. At the time, Norristown had two dams: Norristown Dam and Catfish Dam, below Port Kennedy and Betzwood. Coal waste and agricultural sediments gradually filled the pools behind the dams, and by the late 19th century, canal traffic had virtually come to a halt. The Norristown Dam is maintained by the Philadelphia Electric Company.

Dam at P. & W. R. R. Bridge, Schuylkill River, Norristown, Pa.

216617

14

Catfish Dam was built in 1818 and raised the water level approximately four feet. In 1835 and 1846, the dam was further raised for large cargo vessels. The dam was located below Port Kennedy and Betzwood. In 1951, Catfish Dam was removed during the Schuylkill Dredging Project.

The Schuylkill River has been a source of water supply for municipal waterworks from the early 19th century. In 1847, incorporation of the Norristown Insurance and Water Company to supply water from a central reservoir was approved by the legislature. The city waterworks was located at Barbadoes Street.

THE CANAL SHOWING THE LOCKE IN THE DISTANCE, NORRISTOWN, PA.

In 1828, at a cost of $3 million, a canal system of 108 miles was developed by the Schuylkill Navigation Company. The need to haul coal, lumber, and agricultural produce to the Philadelphia markets stimulated its construction. Approximately 120 locks were located along the canal. By 1932, commercial traffic along the canal ceased. The rapid expansion of rail transportation along the river after the Civil War, and the difficulty in maintaining navigable depths in the slack-water pools due to the silt built up, slowly contributed to the demise of the canal system.

Schuylkill Canal. Norristown. Pa.

216612

Stony Creek, which flows through the borough of Norristown, is one of the three tributaries of the Schuylkill River in Montgomery County. Industries located along the banks of the creek utilized its resources to power mills and factories. By the late 19th century, much of the land along the creek was owned by the Stony Creek Railroad Company, which began service in the 1870s.

On April 14, 1924, the old covered bridge connecting Norristown with Bridgeport at DeKalb Street was destroyed by fire. A four-lane, concrete bridge was soon built to replace the wooden structure at the cost of $500,000.

SCHUYLKILL RIVER BRIDGE LOOKING NORTH, NORRISTOWN, PA.   N-278

The business skyline of Norristown, then and now, is impressive when entering the borough from the Schuylkill River Bridge on DeKalb Street. One can clearly see in these views the county courthouse dome; One Montgomery Plaza, which was the borough's first high-rise office building; St. John's Church; the Valley Forge Hotel, which has long since went the way of the wrecking ball; the Transportation Center; and the spire of the First Presbyterian Church.

SKYLINE OF BUSINESS AREA, NORRISTOWN, PA.   N-282

18

In November of 1689, William Penn ordered Capt. Thomas Holme, his surveyor, to layout a tract of ground on the navigable part of the Schuylkill River. In 1704, Penn gave the land to his son, William, as a gift and called it "Williamstadt." William sold the 7,482-acre property to Isaac Norris and William Trent for 850 pounds. In 1712, Isaac Norris became sole owner of the manor, and the area was called "Norriton" and "Norritingham," derived from Isaac Norris and his descendants.

Interior of DeKalb Street Bridge—Norristown, Pa

A wooden covered bridge spanned the Schuylkill River at DeKalb Street from 1829 until 1924. The bridge was primarily a foot-traffic bridge used by residents until 1924 when it was destroyed by fire. This view is a rare glimpse of the interior of the narrow bridge. On the left side between the vertical beams are barrels.

19

The four steel arches of the Airy Street Bridge spanned Markley Street and the Stony Creek Railroad freight center. This bridge was built in the late 1800s, and a new bridge was constructed in the 1970s. The building on the right is the Pennsylvania Tack Works.

The Norristown Interchange is located off Germantown Pike in Plymouth Meeting. This aerial view of the road system reveals a less developed business area around Plymouth Road; houses line the roadway on Germantown Pike, across the street from the Oasis Bar and Grill. At the time of this picture the Interchange had only two entry and three exit lanes. It has since doubled in size to handle the road traffic.

Two
RIDING THE RAILS

De Kalb Street Station, P&R Railway---Norristown, Pa.

The Philadelphia & Reading Railroad (later called the Reading Railroad) opened for business from Norristown to Philadelphia in 1836. This great view of the DeKalb Station was taken during the centennial celebration in 1912. Note the two shoeshine boys waiting for customers from the incoming train, a young child at the newsstand, a sign for the Western Union telegraph office, and a bicycle leaning against a tour sign.

Originally, the rail lines were constructed for transport of coal, stone, lumber, and other freight. The addition of passenger cars gave people the convenience to work and travel outside of their hometown. This freedom fueled new businesses, increased commerce, and stimulated growth in the community.

At the turn of the 20th century, the Pennsylvania & Reading Railroad made significant investments in branch lines, luxury trains, and elaborate stations for suburban passenger service. This view of the Philadelphia and Reading Norristown Station is an example of one of these elaborate train-station houses. Hotels were often found right next to the train station for the convenience of travelers. On the right is Hotel Windsor.

P. & R. Station, Norristown, Pa.

The Reading Railroad was a multifaceted industrial giant. Originally established as the Philadelphia & Reading Railroad in 1833 to transport anthracite coal, the 94-mile line evolved into a mighty corporation serving eastern Pennsylvania, New Jersey, and Delaware. The P & R helped fuel the Industrial Revolution, which led the United States to economic leadership. With lines reaching out to the north, south, east, and west, the P & R served the heart of the most densely industrialized area of the nation and, by the 1870s, became the largest corporation in the world. Above is the DeKalb Street Station, *c.* 1908, and below is the Transportation Center at Lafayette Street, *c.* 1940.

N7   VIEW OF NORRISTOWN, PA., SHOWING R. R. STATIONS

The Philadelphia & Reading Railroad was chartered in 1833 to serve the coal fields in Pottstown and deliver coal to the city of Reading. Construction was started in 1835; land service began in 1836, by way of horsepower. Early rail vehicles resembled road coaches or wagons, except that the wheels were flanged to fit the tracks. Soon steam engines were used as a source of power to pull the rail wagons. Even though railroads brought development and prosperity to towns along the railway, early citizens had concerns about the neck-breaking train-speeds of 15 miles per hour. Soon, railroads became the dominant mode of transportation, and canal service started to decline. Unlike canals, railroads were not often hampered by ice, snow, or low water and could carry larger loads of freight over longer distances in a shorter time. Several railroad companies had stations in Norristown. These two views are of the Philadelphia and Reading Main Street train station at Main and Markley Streets.

The Pennsylvania Railroad elected to duplicate the Reading's main line in the Schuylkill Valley. By 1884, it had completed a line from West Philadelphia to Norristown. The Pennsylvania Railroad ran numerous trains in the early 1900s, but as the number of automobiles increased, passenger service dwindled. Passenger service was abandoned in 1960. In the *c.* 1914 view above, alongside the train station is Coulston's Garage and Taxi Service. The sign on the building says, "Automobiles for hire all hours." Below is an early view of the same station with Wilson and Walkers Livery stables next to the station. They were in the business of renting and selling carriages, horses, and wagons.

Here is one of the last steam trains of the Pennsylvania Railroad at the Norristown Station. In this 1949 photograph, the train is heading southbound to Philadelphia. It looks like a T-1 Locomotive. The original Reading T-1 Steam Locomotives held 19,000 gallons of water and 21 tons of coal.

Now known as SEPTA's Route 100 Norristown High Speed Line, the Philadelphia and Western, more commonly referred to as the P & W, was built in 1906 from Upper Darby to Strafford. The branch to Norristown, which includes the long truss bridge over the Schuylkill River, was completed in 1912. All-aluminum Bullet cars were the mainstay of this line from 1931 until almost 1990. These high-speed trolleys were the first rail cars designed in a wind tunnel. They were capable of speeds approaching 100 miles per hour and saw 80 miles per hour regularly.

SWEDE STREET, SHOWING ELEVATED OF P. & W. R. R., NORRISTOWN, PA.

Above is a view of the elevated P & W railway that ran along Swede Street crossing over Main Street. The drugstore and restaurant, on the right, served as a terminal for passengers. You would purchase your tickets in the drugstore and go upstairs to the second floor where there was a trolley platform. Below is a close-up view of the P & W "Clock Bridge," which crossed Main Street from Swede. On the left are the Public Square and the Honor Roll Monument. The large white building on the right is the Montgomery Trust Company.

The Honor Roll seen from the Corner of West Main, Norristown, Pa. — 6

25. MAIN STREET, LOOKING WEST, NORRISTOWN, PA.

The P & W railway had an elevated bridge that crossed Main Street and continued along Swede Street near the Public Square. The bridge was often referred to as the Clock Bridge.

Three
A PROSPEROUS COMMUNITY

During the mid-19th century, Norristown was a prominent business community, a center for county government, and home to numerous affluent families. Successful mills and manufacturing centers financed the construction of many elegant mansions and well-built Victorian middle-class homes. Main Street was the center of commercial activity.

East Main Street, Norristown, Pa.

The earliest accommodations for travelers in the 1700s were in private homes. Hosts were only too glad to welcome strangers in return for their company and the news that they brought. As roads and turnpikes developed, inns and taverns were established for profit. Rail travel increased the need for hotels. These establishments sprang up near depots all along the rail lines. The Montgomery Hotel was located on Main Street in Norristown. It was within walking distance of the train station and was also a stop on the trolley line. The hotel was demolished and replaced with a six-story hotel called the Valley Forge Hotel in 1925.

MAIN STREET, NORRISTOWN, PA.

In the early 1900s, goods and services that could not be found in the smaller localities were available in Norristown or Philadelphia. The development of roadways, railroads, and trolley lines gave outlying communities easy access to the amenities offered in the county seat. Norristown was home to several large department stores such as D.M. Yost, Quillman's, Block's, Chatlin's, and Woolworth's. Norristown also had its small "mom and pop" stores. Many operated on a credit system, allowing families to buy on credit and settle the debt when the wage earner received their paycheck.

Main Street in the early 1900s was a hub of activity and business. You would hear the clanging of the trolley as it rocked along the street and the clapping of the horse-drawn wagons. The tall building in the center of this view was the old Times Herald building, the county's local newspaper, which still operates today. Unfortunately a fire demolished this building. Between the Times Herald building and the Norristown Trust Company on the corner was the Grand Opera House.

The Central Norristown Historic District was added to the National Register of Historic Places in 1984. Norristown contains many examples of Greek Revival and Italianate architecture. The district contains historically significant structures built between 1800 and 1924. A variety of these buildings are found in downtown Norristown.

WEST MAIN STREET, SHOWING MASONIC TEMPLE, NORRISTOWN, PA.

The oldest social organizations in Norristown are fraternal orders. The first permanent fraternal lodge in the county was Charity Lodge No. 190, Free and Accepted Masons, organized in 1823 in Norristown. In 1837, the Independent Order of Odd Fellows established its first lodge, Montgomery No. 57, also in Norristown. On the left in this view is the Masonic Temple that was located on west Main Street. The building still stands today.

MAIN STREET, SHOWING HOTEL MONTGOMERY, NORRISTOWN, PA.

In 1900, Norristown had 20 variety stores and 17 dry-good stores. All of these stores could be found in the Boyd's directory. Most took advantage of its very reasonable advertising. The directory was like a telephone book without telephone numbers. It listed businesses, professional practices, industries, and residents. The directory, a must-have in the early 1900s, was published every couple of years.

The B.E. Blocks and Brothers department store of Norristown, founded in 1884 and located on Main Street, survived until the early 1960s. In this view, the old Blocks building is on the left with canopy windows. Both Yost and Blocks fell victim to a sharp decline in business when the enclosed shopping malls came on the scene. Chatlin's Department Store, founded in 1892 and located at 244–252 Main Street, suffered the same fate and closed their doors in 1977.

The D.M. Yost store was the largest store in the county in 1880 and for almost 50 years afterwards. Founded in 1854, Yost was located on the south corner of Main and DeKalb Streets. The store offered a complete line of dry goods, clothing, and household and sewing items. It was a forerunner of the department store. The store survived until about 1960, and the building was then torn down. The stores popularity had a lot to do with the fact that it was located on the corner of the trolley center. Over 100 trolley cars stopped at this corner daily for passengers and to exchange with connecting lines.

Steady immigration and industrial expansion kept builders very busy in Norristown. Much of the town today consists of buildings constructed between 1880 and 1942. As the town expanded outward in all directions, the once open spaces were filled in with row and semidetached homes. Above is a view of Main Street looking west from the corner of Stanbridge Street. Most of this area is still residential, but a few of the homes stretching westward are professional offices. Below is Main Street looking east from around Franklin Avenue. Both views were taken *c.* 1909 when the main means of transportation was horse-drawn wagons and trolleys.

WEST MAIN STREET, NORRISTOWN, PA, LOOKING EAST

Main Street — Norristown, Pa.

Main Street follows an old Indian trail through the Norristown area. The roadway has been known by several other names in its early history, such as "Egypt Road," "Reading Road," the "Perkiomen and Reading Road," and "Ridge Pike." One of the first transportation improvements contributing to the commercial prosperity of Norristown was the construction of the Ridge turnpike. This 24-mile roadway from Philadelphia to the Perkiomen Bridge passed through the borough on a 2-mile stretch along Main Street. The turnpike was started in 1812 and completed in 1816 at the cost of $7,000 per mile.

The message on the back of this card says, "This is a scene of Norristown in Ye Older Times." The card is postmarked May 12, 1912. The view is of the north side of Main Street from below Swede Street to DeKalb Street.

West Main Street -- Norristown, Pa. *n I live right in Back of here E. G. T.*

Many successful entrepreneurs, industrialists, bankers, and physicians built custom homes in the West End of Norristown, reflecting various architectural styles. In the 1920s, real estate brokers began to buy large farms and estates in the West End and in West Norriton in anticipation of residential expansion. The development of small housing communities soon replaced the building of the large custom home. Along the river, Port Indian changed from a summer retreat area to a year-round community. With an ever-growing population in the 1960s came the building of apartment complexes.

RESIDENCE ON MAIN STREET, NORRISTOWN, PA.

MAIN STREET AT DEKALB. NORRISTOWN, PA.   N-280

Norristown was a booming shopping district in the late 1940s, as seen in this view of Main Street near DeKalb Street. By the late 1940s, consumers were demanding greater varieties of products than the traditional general store satisfied. Gradually, regional and national chain stores and specialty shops took root in Norristown. This view is a great time capsule, showing the businesses of that time, such as Triplex Shoes, Morley's, Rogers, the Grand Theater, and the Acme.

This is a linen postcard of Main Street in the 1940s. On the right is the Grand Theater, formally called the Grand Opera House until the arrival of motion pictures. The theater was elaborately decorated, with a gigantic chandelier and plush side-boxes. Opposite the Grand is Woolworth's 5 and 10¢ store.

37

Changes in Norristown's shopping district between the mid–1950s and early 1960s were minimal as evidenced in these two views taken from the same intersection at Main Street and DeKalb Street. The top view dates from *c.* 1961–1962, and the bottom view dates from *c.* 1957. John's Department Store, also remembered a John's Bargain Store, replaced the Grand Theater, and the Paris Shop has replaced Morley's.

Cor. Marshall and Stanbridge Streets, Norristown, Pa.

Most of the residential area was developed between 1880 and World War II. Marshall Street, which runs parallel to Main Street, gets its name from John Marshall, a prominent figure in American history. Stanbridge Street gets its name from John E. Stanbridge, a respected Norristown landowner. On the corner in this view is a small neighborhood grocery store.

Here is a rare look at DeKalb Street south of Main Street. On the left is D.M. Yost's general store, and the tall building belonged to the Independent Order of the Odd Fellows. On the right is a clothing store, and below that was the Schissler College of Business.

Beautiful old homes line the streets of Norristown. The architecture of homes around the town represents a variety of styles that were popular at the various times the homes were built. This view of Swede Street is an example of that diversity. Many of these stately twin homes are professional offices today.

Affluent families built custom homes along the north end of DeKalb Street and the west end of Main Street. Many of these grand homes along DeKalb Street became doctor offices and medical centers because of the homes' proximity to both Sacred Heart and Montgomery Hospitals.

According to the *Schuylkill Valley Atlas,* Stanbridge Street north of Marshall Street was an undeveloped residential area in 1886. However, by 1907, which is the postmark on both of these views, the street was lined with homes on both sides. Originally, the land on the right side of the street was the Bodey Estate, and the property on the left was the S.E. Hartranft Estate. The trolley ran north along Stanbridge to the Stony Creek Rail Station.

Here is a wonderful view of Fornance Street. The street was named after Joseph Fornance, Esq., a prominent resident of Norristown. The homes are decorated with stripped canvas canopies. Canopies were both fashionable and functional. Before air conditioners and electric fans, they helped cool a house by shading the windows.

This is a rare image of a drover herding sheep up Marshall Street. Lewis J. Brendlinger, whose family owned Brendlinger Dry Goods on Main Street, snapped this photograph of Mr. Burns driving the herd in the snow. He was probably taking the herd to the farmers market on Marshall and DeKalb Streets.

This is a classic Main Street view from the 1900s. Main Street was a prosperous retail community. Borough residents and visitors from throughout Montgomery County made frequent visits to downtown Norristown to shop and conduct business affairs. Irwin M. Brendlinger who owned the dry goods store (left) published many great views of Norristown, *c.* 1907. Some of the terrific elements of this view are the open-air trolley, the horse-drawn wagon with the word "Montgomery" written on the side, and the men washing windows on the top floor of the Grand Opera House.

Greeting cards were very popular method for family and friends to keep in touch before the popularity of the telephone. This postal was an invitation for a family in Reading to come join the big celebration in Norristown. "Irma, hope this greeting finds you and your family in good health. Our town is goen to have a big celebration come this May. Hope all of you can come. I will write again with the particulars. JR is feelin much better. Your cousin, Ruth." It sounds as if Ruth was talking about the centennial celebration that was in May of 1912.

Four
WE THE PEOPLE

COUNTY COURT HOUSE, NORRISTOWN, PA.

Montgomery County was created out of part of the Philadelphia County on September 10, 1784. At that same time, Norristown was designated the county seat of government. Norristown hardly existed, even as a tiny village, in 1784. Construction of the first courthouse was completed *c.* 1787 and erected on the northwest corner of the present Public Square. It was a two-story stone structure facing Main Street. The cost was $21,000, including the prison.

By 1849, the first courthouse building was overcrowded, and recommendations were made to build a new one. County commissioners decided to first build a new county prison and then erect a new courthouse. Several feverous debates over moving the county seat arose during the town's early history. In 1851, architect Napoleon LeBrun was commissioned to design the new courthouse and jail. The courthouse extended 196 feet along Swede Street and 64 feet along Airy and Penn Streets. It was constructed of brick and faced with Montgomery County marble. The massive front portico was supported by six columns and was topped by a tower surmounted by a tall spire. The tower was equipped with a clock and bell. The construction was completed in 1854 at a cost of $150,000.

N-9—Public Square showing Monument and County Court House, Norristown, Pa.

In 1876, the courthouse building was remodeled. Gas replaced the kerosene lamps and candles for illumination purposes. Stone cuspidors were placed in the courtrooms, public offices, and in the prisoners' dock. But before the close of the 19th century, it was obvious that the courthouse was inadequate, and plans for a new courthouse were in the works.

CITY HALL, AIRY AND DEKALB STREET, NORRISTOWN, PA.   N-279

City hall located on Airy and DeKalb Streets was built around 1896. This two-story structure was built on the site of the old borough marketplace that stood along DeKalb Street from Airy to Marshall Streets. The first floor was market stalls, and on the second floor were two big halls and borough offices. The building was built of brick in two colors. The main walls were a buff color, and ornamentation was done in red. With age came deterioration. The old city hall was demolished and a new city hall was built on the north side of Airy Street.

PUBLIC SQUARE, NORRISTOWN, PA.

Soldiers' and Sailors' Monument--Norristown, Pa.

The town square, originally owned by the University of Pennsylvania, was conveyed for public use as an open square. It was designated that the square should be kept open forever. There are several monuments of interest still in the square, especially the central obelisk dedicated to Civil War General Zook and the 51st Regiment of Pennsylvania Volunteers. Within the square, farther up Swede Street, is the 1932 Purple Heart Memorial to all Norristonian war casualties.

Court House

A new courthouse was built at a cost of $800,000 and dedicated May 24, 1904. By 1926, planning began for the courthouse annex on the east side of the building. Construction was completed on February 8, 1930. An $11 million expansion project was undertaken in1968. Since that time, several major renovations and expansions have occurred. The interior of the courthouse dates largely from 1904, when the stained glass ceilings in several courtrooms were installed. The murals in courtrooms D and E are by Works Progress Administration (WPA) artist Harding.

There were three attempts to organize a YMCA in Norristown, beginning in 1857. But it was not until 1885 that headquarters were established in the Young Men's Temperance Union Hall. By 1890, the YMCA purchased its own building at 406 DeKalb Street and added a gymnasium. When membership outgrew that facility, the YMCA purchased the former site of the Veranda House, a landmark hotel in Norristown from the late 1800s, and began construction on a new building that included residential rooms, a full gymnasium, and a swimming pool. This location was in operation from 1923 to 1981.

City Hall, Norristown, Pa.

City hall stood on the corner of Airy and DeKalb Streets. It was a great example of Flemish Renaissance architecture. This view shows some of the terrific details of the building, which was built with two different color stones: the main walls were a buff color and a red stone trimmed the windows, doorways, and frame of the building.

Jail, Norristown, Pa.

Since Norristown is the county seat of Montgomery County, county commissioners in 1850 wanted the construction of a new courthouse and jail to portray a county of prosperity and strength. The services of architect Napoleon LeBrun were enlisted to design a magnificent blue marble courthouse and a singularly impressive Gothic jail. The jail is located on Airy Street across from the post office.

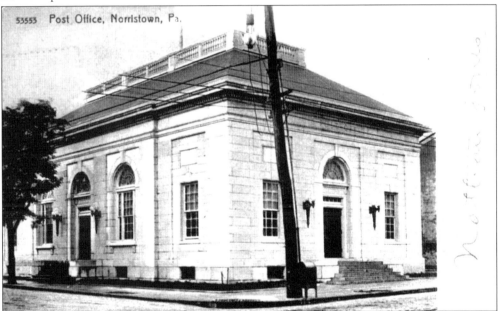

53553 Post Office, Norristown, Pa.

Marble was used as a building material in many government and banking institutions in Norristown. Several quarries located in eastern Montgomery County supplied the stone. This post office, built in 1906, was located at Main and Barbadoes Streets. This is actually the first building the postal service built in Norristown. Until then, the post office had occupied a variety of rented locations over its long history.

U. S. Post Office, Norristown, Pa. — 4

The Norristown post office has occupied several locations in the borough over the years. It has occupied a tavern, a store, a room in the Odd Fellow Hall, and the first floor of the Times Herald Building. In 1906, the postal service decided to erect a marble building at Main and Barbadoes Streets. By 1934, the post office had outgrown this facility, and today's building was erected on Airy Street between DeKalb and Swede Streets. The building is an art deco design by architects James Wetmore and Harry McMurtie. The lobby is adorned with WPA-era murals by Paul Mays.

Montgomery Cemetery on Hartranft Avenue opened in 1848. This large cemetery, about 30 acres, was the first of its kind in the county. Before then, all burials were made in private family plots, church cemeteries, or potter's fields. The cemetery was laid out and sold in lots. Among the five Civil War generals that are buried here are Winfield S. Hancock and John F. Hartranft.

52

Ersine Club House, Norristown, Pa.

Dear friend Mary. Norristown Feb 14/90? Will be pleased to have you come up on Sunday. Your friend. Sara.

After the Civil War, clubs and athletic associations were established to meet the growing demand for recreation in the borough. The Ersine Tennis Club was chartered in 1892 and erected a building with a wide veranda overlooking the tennis courts. The property, located at 1529 DeKalb Street, later became home to the Montgomery County Medical Society.

Moose Building No. 213, Norristown, Pa — 8

The Moose fraternal organization was founded in the late 1800s with the modest goal of offering men an opportunity to gather socially. During the first decade of the 20th century, the Moose reinvented itself into an organization of men and women dedicated to bettering the lives of children and elderly in need and helping their communities on both the national and local level. This was the Moose Lodge in Norristown.

Elks Home, Norristown, Pa.

The oldest social organizations in Norristown are fraternal orders. These fraternities were often referred to as secret societies. They were cloaked in mystic rituals and exotic titles. Most of these societies fostered high moral character, community involvement, and charitable work The Benevolent and Protective Order of Elks of the United States of America is one of the oldest and largest fraternal organizations in the country. Since its inception in 1868, the Order of Elks has grown to include nearly 1.2 million men and women in almost 2,200 communities. They are committed to the ideals of charity and patriotism. This was the Elks Home, Lodge 714, when it was located on West Main Street. Today, the Norristown Chapter meets in Bridgeport. Lodge 714 just celebrated it 100th Anniversary.

Elks No. 714, West Main St, Norristown, Pa — 9

The Veterans of Foreign Wars of the United States traces its roots back to 1899 when veterans of the Spanish-American War (1898) and the Philippine-American War (1899–1902) founded local organizations to secure rights and benefits for their service. There was no medical care or veterans' pension for the sick and wounded that returned from war, and they were left to care for themselves. In their misery, veterans banded together and formed the Veterans of Foreign Wars of the United States. This was the Nuss-O'Hara-Todd Post No. 1804 building in Norristown. Today, there are about 79 members, and the post meets in Bridgeport.

Beginning in April of 1852, regular Meetings for Worship were held here at the Friends' Meetinghouse. Early speakers included Joseph Foulke, noted schoolmaster in Gwynedd, and Lucretia Mott, widely known Quaker preacher and leader in the anti-slavery movement. In 1959, the meetinghouse was remodeled to provide an all-purpose room on the second floor and additional First Day School classrooms. The Friends Meetinghouse is located on Swede and Jacoby Streets.

Abington Friends' Home, Swede & Powell Sts., Norristown, Pa.

The Abington Friends' Boarding Home opened in Norristown in 1897 and served as a retirement home for elderly Quakers for almost 75 years. In 1967, the Friends created a full-care retirement community in Gwynedd called Foulkeways. In 1970, the Abington Friends' Boarding Home in Norristown was closed, and the residents were relocated to Foulkeways.

Copyright 1906 by the Rotograph Co.

A 5764   Gen. Winfield Scott Hancock's old home, Norristown, Pa.

Maj. Gen. Winfield Scott Hancock was born in Montgomery County in 1824 and spent most of his early childhood in Norristown. He was educated at the Norristown Academy, and on the recommendation of the Hon. Joseph Fornance, he was admitted to West Point Military Academy in 1840. He distinguished himself in the Mexican War and later in the Civil War, from which he is referred to as the hero of Gettysburg. Hancock was a presidential candidate in 1880 but lost the election to James Garfield by only 7,000 votes.

The Independent Order of Odd Fellows was a fraternal organization. Their mission was to visit the sick, relieve the distressed, bury the dead, protect the widows of members, and educate orphans. The order's motto was "Friendship, Love, and Truth."

ODD FELLOWS BUILDING
. D. Shafer, 618 W. Marshall St.   Norristown, Pa

The Patriotic Order Sons of America was founded in Philadelphia in 1845. The organization was a fraternal society that claimed to trace its lineage to the Sons of Liberty, a Revolutionary War order founded in Boston. In the 1880s, the Patriotic Order Sons of America helped the Valley Forge Centennial and Memorial Association purchase Washington's Headquarters in Valley Forge. This postcard is a picture of the Fred E. Stees, Commandery No. 18 members from Norristown.

This view shows one of the floats from the Historical Day Parade during the town's 1912 centennial celebration. The float was titled "Fete at William Moore Smith's 1784." William Moore Smith was the first provost of the University of Pennsylvania. Under the direction of the university in 1784, he was entrusted with the task of planning out the town, and he named it Town of Norris. The Countles Gas Company sponsored the float. The Druggists Association donated the horses, and the re-enactors were from the First Presbyterian Church.

91. WHO SAID RACE SUICIDE?

A SAMPLE LOT OF NORRISTOWN BABIES.

The history, character, and charm of Norristown has been built on the ethnic diversity of its population. From incorporation to the start of the Civil War, Norristown's population grew in leaps and bounds due largely to immigrants looking for work, prosperity, and freedom. Bursting at the seams, the borough expanded its boundaries again in 1853. The steady growth in this diverse population gave rise to many new churches and social organizations.

58

Five
BUSINESS AS USUAL

The Montgomery Insurance, Trust, and Safe Deposit Company was chartered April 24, 1884. On May 20, 1905, the name was change to Montgomery Trust Company. This grand Romanesque-style building with its tall columns stood on Main Street near the Public Square. Like many grand financial institutions of the time, the interior was adorned with marble floors, fine woods, and brass railings. The architect was Benjamin Rush Stevens from Philadelphia.

In 1874, when the first theater, or opera house as they were commonly known, was built in Norristown, it was called the "Music Hall." These halls were never really built for operas but were used for community meetings, social functions, concerts, and eventually, plays, vaudeville shows, and movies. Norristown had several early theaters: the Garrick Theater, the Grand Opera House, the New Music Hall, the Bijou, the Westmar, and the Norris to name a few. The Garrick and the Westmar were eventually torn down to make way for a gas station and parking lot. Others became lumberyards, office centers, and even apartment houses.

Garrick Theatre, Norristown, Pa.

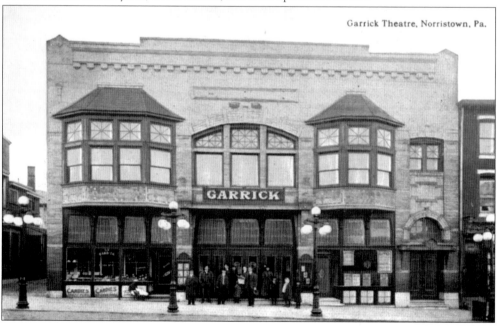

Norristown Service Garage

Ira G. Singleton. Prop.

When automobiles rolled off the assembly lines into towns, the auto mechanic and service station were born. If you were wealthy enough to afford a car, you also had to be handy enough to fix it. A ride in the country often meant a walk home or a tow back by a local farmer's horse. Early auto mechanics were often machine mechanics. Ira G. Singleton, a machine mechanic by trade, stands in front of his Norristown Service Garage. The view is dated September 10, 1918.

W.K. Gresh & Sons cigar factory was located on Marshall Street just west of Markley Street. The plant comprised two large buildings that housed the cigar plant, powerhouse, box factory, printing plant, machine shop, and office. The plant at one point employed about one thousand workers. Gresh's nickel and dime cigars were marketed nationwide. Today, the buildings are still standing; one was renovated into an apartment building.

Farmers Hotel and Post Office, Norristown, Pa.

In the late 1880s, the Farmers Hotel was located on Main Street at the corner of Barbadoes Street. The proprietor, at that time, was Hiram Beerer. The hotel had stable accommodations for livestock and horses. This was an added convenience for drovers who would bring livestock to market.

The railroad was pivotal in the growth of Norristown and the need for good lodging. Catering to the weary travelers, early hotels were located within walking distance of the railway. The Central Hotel and Café was located at 200 Main Street. E.S. Shelly was proprietor at the time of this view.

Lanz's Jewelry Store at 211 DeKalb Street was a retail landmark for fine jewelry, diamonds, and silverware in Norristown. Gustave Lanz was a diamond merchant and established the store in 1878. Lanz's had a reputation for fine quality and reasonable prices. The store was exquisitely decorated with tall cherry wood display cases. Both of these views are great advertising postcards of the interior of the store. The variety of merchandise can be seen on the shelves and in the cases.

GUSTAVE LANZ
Diamond Merchant & Jeweler
211 DeKalb Street, Norristown, Pa.

Established 1878

Tom's Gulf Service Station was located on East Main and Franklin Streets. Self service did not exist at the time this advertising card was printed. In fact, these were the days when the service attendant wore a clean white uniform and never left you waiting at the pump.

How rare it is today to see a bar stocked like this one. Tutt's Place was a very popular neighborhood bar owned by Harry Singleton on Stanbridge and Washington Streets. The establishment offered 760 different brands of liquor and 115 different brands of beer from which to choose. Top shelf, literally meant the best was on the top shelf and required a stepstool to reach it. At the time of this advertising postcard, drinks ranged from 10¢ to $1.00.

Now available for immediate delivery at the new reduced prices.

Marchese's was a well-known automobile dealership in Norristown for decades. This postcard is of the Marchese GMC Truck Sales and Service location that was at Basin and Cherry Streets. At the time this advertising card was mailed to potential customers, these were new trucks.

This is a rare interior view of "The Cabin." This was a public dinning area inside the Valley Forge Hotel. Its rustic décor made one feel as if they were in the Poconos not Norristown. The Valley Forge Hotel opened in 1925. Unfortunately, it was destroyed to erect a parking garage.

Bowling has a long and rich history and, today, is one of the most popular sports in the world. In the late 1950s and 1960s, bowling lanes also served as a social center for teens and young adults. Trooper Bowling Lanes on Ridge Pike in Trooper was a great place to meet friends and enjoy the game.

Famous for its home cooking and businessmen's luncheon, the Ream's Hotel was located on Penn and Swede Streets, opposite the courthouse. In the late 1880s, it was known as the Rambo House.

Jarrett Livery and Boarding Stables on Jacoby and Willow Streets was owned and operated by John Jarrett. Jarrett Livery was known for its first-class horse teams. Teams and carriages were rented for weddings, funerals, outings, and business travel. In 1902, a horse and carriage rental was $1.50 a day.

With the birth of the automobile came the desire to travel and take to the open road. Motels or motor courts offered long-distance travelers a clean bed and an affordable meal. Obie's Place was located just north of Route 73 on Route 202. Accommodations were considered top notch with automatic thermostat heating, televisions, radios, Beautyrest box springs and mattresses, private baths, and cross ventilation.

TWENTY-THIRD YEAR

We have one of the best schools in Pennsylvania, and will return to any student who shall enter every cent of tuition paid, if, after one month's trial, he fails to agree with us. A fair investigation and an honest judgment is all we ask. Positions guaranteed graduates or money refunded. Write for free catalogue giving full particulars. Fall term begins August 29th, 1910.

Schissler College of Business
NORRISTOWN, PENNA.

Aloysius J. Schissler founded Schissler College of Business in 1887. This educational institution was dedicated to preparing students for the world of business. The college was very successful during the late 1800s and early 1900s. Job placement was guaranteed to graduates or their money was refunded. The college was located on Main and DeKalb Streets, but as enrollment increased, the college purchased several properties along DeKalb Street and expanded the school.

Several Textile companies were located in Norristown in the late 1800s. These companies employed thousands of area residents. The Wyoming Spinning Company was located on Swede Street; the company was known for their quality yarns. The Eureka Knitting Company, also located at the foot of Swede Street, was known for its ribbed underwear for women. The Globe Knitting Mills, known for producing superior hosiery, was located on Moore and Walnut Streets and founded in 1885 by Joseph Rambo and George Lee. Shortly after the founding of the company, George Lee left, and on September 1, 1886, H.R. Regar became a partner. Production soon outgrew the facility on Moore and Walnut Streets, and a larger site was purchased on Main Street between Chester and Ford Streets. The construction of a state-of-the-art building was completed in 1898. This new site was built on the former location of the Mary Cresson Woolen Factory.

With the increased popularity and affordability of automobiles, traveling became an American pastime. Motor courts sprang up all over the country along well-paved highways. Charley's Motor Court was located on Route 202, three miles to the north of Norristown. It was owned and operated by Charles Freas.

The Log Cabin was an upscale restaurant located north of Norristown on Route 202. "Food that excels" and "Rendezvous of Distinction" were the descriptions used for the advertisement of this establishment. Ownership has changed hands several times over the years. Today, the restaurant is not in operation.

The General DeKalb Inn, now known as the Jefferson House Restaurant, was formally the mansion house of William Buckland, a Norristown manufacturer. Originally built in 1848, the home was partially destroyed by fire in 1920. Architect Mantle Fielding, influenced by Thomas Jefferson's Monticello, rebuilt the home. This stately Georgian-style building was fully restored and still operates as a showcase restaurant with views overlooking the lush foliage of landscaped grounds. The gardens have a duck pond, a 150-year old springhouse, a fountain, and Italian gazebos. This picturesque setting is located on DeKalb Pike south of Germantown Pike. The restaurant is currently being remolded as a result of a fire.

The Hotel Hartranft, also known as the Hartranft House, was located at 245 West Main Street within walking distance of the Main Street train depot. Often the address of a hotel was advertised with regards to its location to the train or trolley station. While hotels catered to travelers coming to the county seat or larger manufacturing centers by rail, they did not neglect farmers and drovers. Virtually every hotel had a livery stable with good hostlers.

VALLEY FORGE HOTEL, NORRISTOWN, PA   2935.29

The Valley Forge Hotel was an elegant hotel built in 1925. It was constructed on the site of the old Montgomery House, which stood opposite the courthouse on Main Street. The hotel was six stories high and had 82 rooms, a public and private dinning room, ballroom, meeting room, a grill, and a variety of other services. It was the largest hotel in the county when it was built. This postcard of the hotel (on left) boasts the $2.50 room rate that of course did not include a bath. Due to a decline in business, the hotel was demolished so a parking garage could be erected.

VALLEY FORGE HOTEL

NORRISTOWN, PENNSYLVANIA

The Hotel Hamilton was located on the corner of Hamilton and West Main Streets. It was the first apartment building in the West End of Norristown. The Hamilton was intended as living quarters for bachelors and transient guests. This landmark was replaced by a modern apartment building called the Hamilton Apartments.

CROSS ROADS MOTEL

With the increased use of cars in the 1930s, hotels and inns no longer needed to be near train stations or trolley lines. Private tourist houses were opened to travelers for overnight lodging, and a few tourist courts were constructed. After the completion of the Pennsylvania Turnpike in the late 1940s, motels sprang up along the major roadways. The Cross Roads Motel was located at the intersection of Route 202 and Township Line Road. Today, this site is now a shopping center.

J.S. Connelly was a wholesale dealer of farm machinery and motor vehicles in Norristown. His home, Oak Lawn Stock Farm, was located on Germantown Pike. This postcard is from 1909, and from the looks of the size of the barn, business must have been very good. Notice the images of cows on the fence and someone fishing at the lake.

Bungalow Inn
Route 422, Ridge Pike
Jeffersonville, Pa.

The Bungalow Inn was a restaurant, bar, and banquet hall on Ridge Pike, west of Burnside Avenue, across the street from the golf course. It was owned and operated by Joseph B. Uhler at the time of this postcard. The building was later demolished. Today, a gym and Italian restaurant are located here.

Norristown Trust, later known as Penn Trust and Norristown Penn Trust, was incorporated on August 21, 1888. A location was secured, and an impressive financial icon was built at the corner of Main and DeKalb Streets, convenient to both the trolley and railroad lines. This location was the former site of Yeakle's store on Main Street and the Barnes Estate on DeKalb. This five-story building was constructed of brick with limestone trimmings and had a frontage on Main Street of 50 feet and a depth of 96 feet on DeKalb. The view above dates from *c.* 1906 and the view on the right dates from *c.* 1930.

NORRISTOWN PENN TRUST CO., NORRISTOWN, PA.

The People's National Bank and Trust Company was chartered October 25, 1881, as People's National Bank of Norristown. Its home originally was the Jamison mansion until 1905. The mansion was torn down, and a new bank was built. The banks original capital was $100,000.

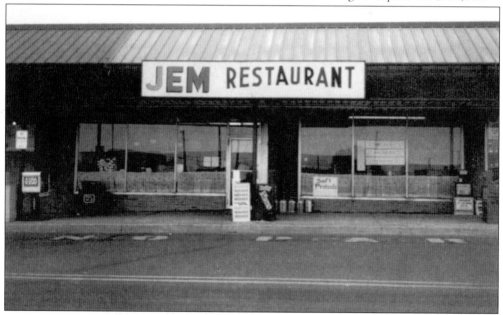

Jem's restaurant needs no introduction to locals from East Norriton and the surrounding area. Hundreds of people go to Jem's for good food and great service. Proof of this can be seen on the weekends when a breakfast line starts forming 10 minutes before the restaurant opens. Toni and Linda Bello have owned and operated Jem's for over 30 years. The interior of the restaurant is a 1950s motif with great pictures and nostalgic items hanging on the wall. Jem's is located in the Swede Square shopping center on Swede Road and Germantown Pike.

Here is a great novelty card postmarked 1914. The message is appropriate: " Sorry, I had to leave without saying goodbye. But something came up and I had to rush off. Hope you're not upset with me. See you in a couple of weeks."

The first floor in old city hall was a marketplace, similar to today's farmers markets. The market attracted hundreds of people, who would come to town to by supplies and sell produce. Dora E. Seeley was manager at the time of this antique show.

The Adam Scheidt Brewing Company was founded in the late 1870s and was incorporated in 1884. After Prohibition, the brewery thrived, brewing Valley Forge Beer, Ram's Head Ale, and Prior Beer. The brewery's name was changed to the Valley Forge Brewing Company in 1963, and five years later, it was sold to C. Schmidt & Sons. It continued to operate as a branch of Schmidt's until 1975 when the facility was closed. Schmidt's continued to brew the Valley Forge and Ram's Head brands until the early 1980s when Schmidt's itself ceased operations. The brewing facility was demolished. This is one of the office buildings on Markley Street that is still standing.

The *Norristown Times Herald* has been around since the first criers walked Main Street in Norristown calling out the headlines of the *Norristown Gazette*. The paper can trace its history back to 1799. The *Times Herald* has been a steady source of national, international, and local news for more then 200 years. Here is a birthday greeting postcard for a member of the "Fifty Year Club." Postmark on the card is 1942.

Six

HOMETOWN HEROES

This is the team of horses that raced with an auto and won on Thanksgiving Day H. Karnes

HANCOCK CHEMICAL ENGINE CO., NO. 5, NORRISTOWN, PA.

In 1813, concerned citizens of Norristown pioneered the first firefighting group. Most early firefighting efforts were bucket brigades. By the late 1800s, Norristown had five fire companies protecting its citizens: the Norristown Hose Company (known as the Norris) and the Montgomery Fire Company were chartered in 1848; the Humane Fire Company in 1887, the Fairmount Fire Company in 1852, and the Hancock Chemical Engine Company in 1895.

Hancock Chemical Fire Engine Co. No. 5, Norristown, Pa.

In the 1890s, the use of chemicals instead of water was introduced as a new firefighting method. Residents in the West End wanted a chemical fire engine to eliminate the damage that was being caused by heavy streams of water. At a meeting in Western Hall Market on November 21, 1895, the Hancock Chemical Fire Company was organized. A three-story firehouse was built on Airy Street near Stanbridge Street. The Hancock firehouse was dedicated on Thanksgiving Day, 1896, and a firemen's parade was held. The parade tradition continued on Thanksgiving Day for many years.

HANCOCK ENGINE COMPANY, NORRISTOWN, PA.

The Fairmount Fire Company was organized on February 22, 1852, and incorporated on May 19, 1853. The establishment of the Fairmount Fire Company was in response to the growing West End population. The firehouse is located on Main and Astor Streets.

FAIRMOUNT H. AND L. COMPANY, OF NORRISTOWN, PA.

The Humane Fire Engine Company was established in 1852. The company constructed a station house on Airy Street above DeKalb Street in 1854. Later, a new firehouse was erected on Main and Green Streets. To the left, the station house has been decorated for the town's centennial celebration that was held in 1912. The gentlemen on the corner are probably waiting for the parade to pass the firehouse. Note the spectator on the roof of the building. He *really* had a bird's eye view of the festivities.

In November of 1847, a public meeting was held at the Montgomery Hotel to organize a volunteer fire company. The Norristown Fire Company was formed. The first location secured for the station house was 417 DeKalb Street. The new building was dedicated in 1848. The Norris Fire Company, as it is often called, quickly grew, and from 1852–1854, this location housed two active fire companies while the Humane firehouse was under construction. By 1857, the original site was sold, and property was purchased on the east side of DeKalb Street above Airy Street. On this site, they erected a three-story building and housed their first steam fire engine, an Amoskeag Pumper. After 24 years, the Norris had outgrown its station again. At a meeting on January 7, 1881, it was decided that a building lot would be purchased at the corner of Chestnut and DeKalb Streets to build again.

The site at Chestnut and DeKalb Streets for the new Norris Fire Company station was met with opposition by some of the local residents. Nevertheless, the company built a three-story station house. The building was dedicated in 1883. By 1949, the structure was in severe need of renovation; the third floor was no longer suitable and was closed. The company contemplated moving again to a site at DeKalb and Jacoby Streets, but the Norristown Board of Adjustment vetoed the plan. Renovations began in 1950, and the third floor was removed.

A fire often attracted a lot of attention. Crowds of spectators would gather to watch the firemen in action. Montgomery Hose Company and Norristown Fire Company are the two oldest fire companies still in existence in Norristown. Both were organized within days of the other in 1847. The members that joined the Montgomery Hose Company were dissatisfied with the formation of the Norristown Fire Company and therefore established their own company. They received their charter on June 10, 1848, and in that same year built a building on Penn Street. In 1911, Montgomery Hose got its first motorized chemical engine truck.

The "Montgomery" of Norristown, Pa.

Of course no parade is complete without a marching band. Here are two views of the Norris Hose Company members and their band members. The band members besides being firemen were probably members of the Norristown Band or the Liberty Band. Both bands were very popular in the early 1900s. A parade celebration was the best time to get a group picture. Parading was almost as important as firefighting for early firemen. When a company dedicated a new firehouse, there was a big parade with numerous visiting companies. The purchase of new equipment also gave cause for a parade and celebration. Silver parade horns were often given as gifts from visiting companies in recognition of hospitality. These parade horns were prized possessions of a fire company and were carried proudly under the arm of the marshal as the company paraded.

The Centennial Firemen's Day Parade was held on Thursday, May 9, 1912. Justice of the peace Oliver F. Lenhart was chief marshal, assisted by Theodore Lane Bean, Esq. This was, to that date, the largest parade by firemen ever held in Montgomery County. No less then 72 of the county's fire companies marched to the tune of brass bands along the two-mile pageant route. Thousands of spectators lined the streets to cheer these brave volunteers.

Liberty Fire Co., Reading—Taken at Norristown, Thanksgiving Day, 1908

Norristown hosted the state firemen's convention in 1894, and 4,000 firemen and scores of equipment paraded the streets. The first Thanksgiving Day Parade held in town was in 1897 when Fairmount Fire Company dedicated its new house. In 1903, 35 outside fire companies were invited to join the Norristown Thanksgiving Day Parade. This is a view of the Liberty Fire Company from Reading on the steps of the courthouse. They joined Norristown's parade celebration in 1908.

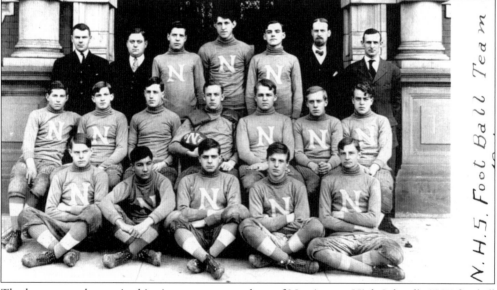

The hometown heroes in this picture were members of Norristown High School's 1907 football team. The first football game was played at Oakview Park in 1892. It featured teams from the high school and the YMCA. Norristown won 14-4. The high school's early teams were frequently sponsored by one of the town's athletic clubs.

Seven

TURNING
ONE HUNDRED

In 1912, Norristown had reached its 100th year since incorporation. In preparation for this milestone, the town planned a historical pageant. Buildings along the parade route and throughout town were finely decorated with American flags, red, white, and blue banners and other patriotic ephemera. The parade route along Main Street was lined with tall white columns, earning the name "Court of Honor."

The centennial celebration began on Sunday, May 5, 1912, with special services in all the town's churches. Later that afternoon, there was a town meeting held at the Grand Opera House. Each day that week was dedicated to an important segment of Norristown history. The first day of the pageant's many parades was Monday, Municipal and Educational Day. Gov. John K. Tener and Philadelphia Major Blankenburg were the guests of honor. Civic Day was observed on Tuesday, Wednesday was Industrial Day, Thursday was Firemen's Day, Friday was Historical Day, and Saturday was Military Day.

Local newspapers of the day reported daily on the pageantry of the centennial celebration. The *Norristown Times* wrote, "A two-mile pageant, gorgeous in costuming, rich in historical lore, of great educational value, and interesting in its personnel and characteristics, marked Historical Day." The *Norristown Daily Herald* said, "The pageant was superb. It was a spectacle which will linger long in the memory of every man, women and child who witnessed it." The *Norristown Daily Register* said, "The pageant was highly instructive and made a firm and lasting impression upon every one of the thousands who witnessed it."

The school pageant with thousands of children in costumes must have been an impressive sight. All of the town's schools, public and parochial, participated in the Educational Day Parade. Many of the costumes were handmade by students, women's clubs, and parents.

The students in this picture were from the Cherry Street School. Hundreds of spectators turned out for all the parades, but most of the people along the parade route in this picture were probably proud parents and family members. The Cherry Street School was built in 1852 and operated until 1939.

Norristown High School students represented some of their school clubs in the parade. In this view, the Science and Art Clubs are passing the First Methodist Episcopal Church on DeKalb Street. In the background, two spectators have climbed the electric pole to get a better view.

Standing outside St. Patrick's Church are the school's elementary students waiting to take their place in the Educational Day procession. Thousands of children from the borough marched, representing their schools.

The centennial celebration was a week of splendid celebrations. These Norristown residents took a few minutes to pose for a group photograph on this auspicious occasion.

During the centennial parade, merchants decorated their establishments with flags, buntings, and banners to express their community support and involvement in the celebration. Some of the businesses in this view are the Norristown Supply Company, Keystone Garage, and the Ideal Burial Company. Take note of the man, at the left of the picture, raising the roof on his convertible.

During the centennial celebration of 1912, Norristown illuminated the two-mile parade route with strings of electric lights. This was a significant display for a town in 1912 that still had many kerosene and gas street lamps, which remained until 1915. Above is a unique night view of city hall illuminated with a large "welcome" sign. Below is Main Street's Court of Honor decorated with strings of lights. It was not until October 1884 that a group of Norristown merchants organized the Norristown Electric Light and Power Company. Two months later, the Norristown Excelsior Electric Light Company was started. At first, only arc lights were used for streets and stores, but soon incandescent lamps made electric lights suitable for the home. In 1893, the Norristown Gas Company acquired control of the Norristown Electric Light and Power Company. Subsequent mergers placed the Philadelphia Electric Company in control.

Not only were citizens of Norristown out in force to celebrate the 100th anniversary of their town but also so were thousands of visitors from all parts of the county. Family, friends, and spectators from Philadelphia came to witness this momentous occasion. Norristown was ready to impress the public and leave a lasting impression during their centennial parade celebration. Above is a great view of the People's National Bank. To the right of the bank is the Music Hall, and to the left is the Box Ball Bowling Parlor. Norristown had several early commercial bowling lanes in the borough. On the left is the Montgomery Trust Company.

There are more than 1,000 postcards printed of the centennial parades in 1912. Especially great ones are those of Main and DeKalb Streets. Views, like these, are time capsules of life at the turn of the 20th century. Some of these historic buildings are gone, but the clarity of these pictures brings everything back to life again. Above is the Hotel Windsor at DeKalb and Washington Streets. The hotel was conveniently located near the DeKalb Street train station. The banner over the street is done in lights. It says "1910 Population 28000" and "Watch us Grow—Norristown, the Place to Live." There is a sign on the wall of the hotel advertising Scheidt Beer—10¢. The car passing the hotel has the steering wheel on the right-hand side. Below is Main Street with a horse-drawn wagon; on the side of the wagon is printed Norris Laundry. At Lovatt's Drug Store you can read the word grape juice on the storefront window. The wagon is stationed outside Childs near the Penn Hotel.

97

All of the borough's civic organizations and societies participated in the centennial pageant. The Loyal Order of the Moose, Lodge 213 officers can be seen here in this picture riding in an unusual motor vehicle. Take note of the large moose in the middle of the truck towering above the driver. Other members of the lodge are in procession alongside the vehicle.

B.E. Block & Bros. sponsored many beautiful floats in the centennial pageant of 1912. This float advertised "Old Hickory, the ideal porch furniture." On the float are several handmade rockers. Inside the flower-laced gazebo are three little faces peeking out. The woman on the float is probably a Block's employee, and you can barely see the wagon driver to the right amidst all the flowers. Even these beautiful white horses are decorated with garland.

Eight
A WALK IN THE PARK

Norristown's principle recreational area is Elmwood Park. It was opened in 1908, after Amos W. Barnes gifted about 35 acres of the former Scott farm to the borough. At the time, it was simply a wooded area boarding Stony Creek. Over the years, various recreational facilities have been added to the park, and still today, it is enjoyed by thousands of residents.

BOULEVARD, ELMWOOD PARK, NORRISTOWN, PA.

Harding Boulevard looks much different today. Homes line the roadway opposite Elmwood Park. This is a view of the Boy Scout cabin that was a gift from the Norristown Rotary Club.

A Scene in Elmwood Park, Norristown, Pa. A-342

Elmwood Park, so named because of the towering elm trees that blanket the landscape, was a popular place with the young men and women of the town in the 1900s. It gave them a public place to socialize. The men would often gather for a game of ball, and the young ladies would stroll the park hoping for a chance encounter with their beau.

Elmwood Park's scenic view along Stony Creek was a popular spot for residents, visitors, and postcard photographers. There are plenty of different views of the park and of Stony Creek available today.

Before there was television, video games, indoor arcades, and air-conditioning, you could not keep a child indoors. There was always plenty to do, adventures to be had, and treasures to be found at Elmwood Park. These three little adventurers are taking a break in the shade on the bridge from the afternoon sun.

RUSTIC BRIDGE, ELMWOOD PARK, NORRISTOWN

Social outings at Elmwood Park were commonplace. Many of the local churches used the park for picnics and choir concerts. The women posing on the bridge are dressed in their Sunday best with beautifully decorated hats. A gentlemen escort stands on the bridge gazing at Stony Creek.

The Fire Chiefs Memorial Band Shell was dedicated in 1936 as a memorial to former Norristown fire chiefs. It is located in Elmwood Park and still hosts summer Sunday evening concerts in the park. At the time of the dedication, those honored were John Slingluff, the first fire chief who served from 1896 to 1899; Peter V. Hoy, from 1899 to 1932; and George W. Pifer, from 1932 to 1935.

Thousands of Norristown residents gathered at Elmwood Park for Dedication Day in 1908. Local civic organizations and several of the area churches sponsored activities for a day filled with good food and fun. Above is a view of residents gathering for the dedication ceremonies. On this summer Sunday afternoon, the men are dressed in suits and hats. The women are finely attired in long dresses and bonnets. It was customary in the early 1900s for both men and women to were hats in public. Below is a group of children enjoying the hot summer day with a tub race on the lake. It looks as if the spectators are cheering them on to the finish line.

Tub Race on the Lake
Dedication Day

In 1924, Elmwood Park opened the Elmwood Zoo. Although the zoo was small, it attracted visitors from around the county. In 1985, the Borough of Norristown, which had operated the zoo since it opened, turned over operations to the private, non-profit Norristown Zoological Society. The zoo doubled its size from 8 to 16 acres, and new animal exhibits were added. The Andrew L. Lewis Wetlands and Aviary, which opened in 1995, was among the first of the new exhibits. The indoor bayou exhibit of American reptiles and amphibians was opened in 1996. In May 1997, a new million dollar entrance pavilion and parking complex was opened, and in August 1997, Phase I of the Grasslands Exhibit was opened with two young female bison and a young female elk. The Powell Pavilion was completed in 1999, and Phase II of the Grasslands Exhibit will open in 2002. The zoo hosts special events all season long.

The Monkeys at Elmwood Park, Norristown, Pa. — 3

BARTHOLD'S ORCHESTRA
JOHN E. BARTHOLD, CONDUCTOR, 137 W. AIRY ST., NORRISTOWN

Outside of Philadelphia, orchestras did not enjoy the same popularity as bands in the 1900s. Classical music was popular in affluent social circles. This is a postcard of the Barthold Orchestra from Norristown.

Samuel Stephens was a prolific composer, conductor, and musician. Several of his compositions were played by John Phillip Sousa's band. He founded the Norristown Boys' Band, also known as the Stephens Juvenile Band, in 1914. The group won statewide recognition and traveled to many engagements consistently winning honors. The band began with 44 boys and grew to 60 boys ranging in age from 7 to 14. Stephens was also a successful entrepreneur. He owned and operated a music store called "Stephens' House of Music" on Main Street opposite the Garrick Theatre.

One of the most popular forms of musical entertainment in the early 1900s was the brass marching band. Such bands were ideal entertainment for parades, church socials, fire engine housings, holiday celebrations, and special community festivities. This is the St. Patrick's Parish Band. The band played for parish and community functions. The boys ranged from 7 to 17 years of age. They must have made an impressive appearance in these uniforms.

Nine
IN SERVICE TO
THE COMMUNITY

The Missionary Sisters of the Most Sacred Heart of Jesus founded Sacred Heart Hospital in 1936 as an acute-care general hospital. The hospital had 40 beds in a converted home on the corner of DeKalb and Fornance Streets. When increasing demands made it necessary, other homes were purchased to expand services. In 1978, the hospital underwent major reconstruction. The building is now the home of Montgomery County Human Services.

Montgomery Hospital is the oldest general hospital in Southeastern Pennsylvania, outside of Philadelphia, to provide healthcare for Norristown and its surrounding communities. At the time of its founding, the closest hospital was in Philadelphia, a day's travel away. Accidents in the quarries, mills, and factories in the area demanded immediate medical attention. The original hospital was located in a vacant school at Powell and Basin Streets in Norristown. Originally named Charity Hospital, the hospital opened its doors on January 1, 1891, with a staff of six. The hospital's modern history began with its 50th anniversary in 1939 when the first section of today's existing building was completed. By 1978, the hospital grew to a total of 265 beds. A parking garage was added in 1985, and a professional building was constructed in 1986 to house physician offices, the Montgomery Cancer Center, and the Medical Center's rehabilitation wing. The hospital campus is situated on 4.1 acres and located at 1301 Powell Street at the junction of Powell and Fornance.

Charity Hospital, Norristown, Pa.

Issued by F. D. SHAFFER, 518 W. Marshall St.

108

Before 1876, the mentally ill of Montgomery County were cared for in almshouses in Philadelphia. These facilities were inadequate and severely overcrowded. To address this problem, a mental healthcare facility was built in Norristown. On July 12, 1880, the State Hospital for the Insane (now Norristown State Hospital) opened its doors.

The 92 acres of rural agricultural land near the Stony Creek Railroad Station were chosen for the state mental hospital because of the land's accessibility to Philadelphia and neighboring counties. Civil War Gen. John F. Hartranft chaired the board of trustees.

On July 12, 1880, the State Hospital for the Insane at Norristown admitted the first 400 male patients. Women were accepted in 1883 when Building One was completed. Later construction included the Dr. Joseph Thomas Laboratory (1905), the Assembly Hall with seating for 1,000 (1909), a new admission building (1934), and the Arthur P. Noyes Library building (1954).

The period of greatest growth for the state hospital followed the appointment of Dr. Arthur P. Noyes as superintendent from 1936 to 1959. With Noyes as director, the hospital became a major psychiatric training center, utilizing the latest approved teaching and treatment methods.

State Hospital, Showing Administration Building and Doctors' Offices, Norristown, Pa.

Shortly after beginning operations, the staff at the state hospital noticed that residents of the hospital assigned to daily chores were happier and easier to manage. With outside personnel as overseers, patients maintained the grounds, worked on the farm, serviced the laundry, and worked in many other areas of the hospital. Many patients learned trades.

Here is a rare interior view of Assembly Hall at the Norristown State Hospital. The hall had a tremendous seating capacity of about 1,000 people. The hall is decorated with fall ornaments such as the cornhusks hanging from the rafters. The tables are covered with white linen tablecloths, place settings, and ceramic water pitchers. This may actually be a view of the dinning hall before Thanksgiving dinner.

Section One - one of the many buildings of the Hospital. Alice.

Glad to hear from you.
L. A. W.

Norristown State Hospital was established on a rural agricultural site in 1879 and opened its doors as the regional psychiatric hospital for eastern Pennsylvania in 1880. By the turn of the 20th century, over 4,000 patients were being treated at Norristown for major mental illnesses. Men and women received treatment in separate facilities at the hospital. They even had separate pharmacies and autopsy rooms. The administration building was the demarcation point separating these facilities. Building One was the first building constructed for female patients.

STATE HOSPITAL OPERA COMPANY. Season 1908-9 Norristown. Pa.

Restraints were forbidden, and personal rights and self-respect were encouraged as part of the hospital policy. Social functions such as dances, concerts, picnics, and plays were held regularly at the hospital. Patients were encouraged to participate and organize these functions. Here is a picture of the State Hospital Opera Company from the 1908–1909 season.

Montgomery Hospital, Norristown, Pa. — 10

Montgomery Hospital began in 1889 and opened its doors as Charity Hospital of Montgomery County. In 1920, the name was changed to Montgomery Hospital, and in 1938, construction of the new hospital began. The $650,000 building had 134 beds, 28 bassinets, and centralized medical services. Today, the hospital has grown to a total of 265 beds and sits on 4.1 acres of ground in the heart of Norristown. It has a parking garage, professional building, a cancer center, and medical rehabilitation center. The hospital continues to grow and provide the area residents and communities with the best care available.

Chain Street
School and
John F.
Hartranft
School

Norristown,
Pa.

The Chain Street schoolhouse, built in 1870, was located at the corner of Chain and Airy Streets. It was a two-story building with eight rooms, each room accommodating about 50 children. Adjacent to it was the John F. Hartranft School, located between Chain and George Streets, near Airy, and built in 1894. Both schools were destroyed in the early 1950s for the construction of the new Hartranft School, which was dedicated in 1952. The school closed in 1977 because of a drop in student population.

23 GEORGE WASHINGTON PUBLIC SCHOOL, NORRISTOWN, PA.

The George Washington School was built in 1922 at High and Marshall Streets in the east end of Norristown. It was planned as a junior high school but was used as an elementary school instead. A large four-room addition was added to the school in 1928, but with the decline of enrollment, the school closed in 1969 and was rented to Montgomery County for day-care operations.

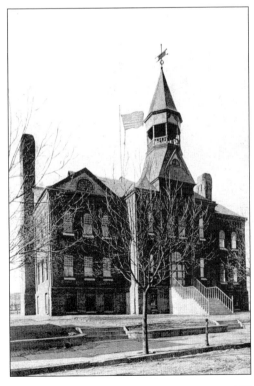

The Noble Street School was built in 1888, on Noble below Marshall Street. It could accommodate 380 students and was fully occupied by the fall of 1889. In 1913, it was destroyed by fire but was rebuilt the same year. In 1921, the name was changed to the Lincoln School. The school was enlarged in 1962 but closed in 1977 due to a decline in enrollment.

Norristown High School began as the DeKalb Street School in 1880, and the building was enlarged in 1899. This building closed in 1938, and students were transferred to the new A.D. Eisenhower Senior High School.

In 1935, the school board purchased 9.54 acres from the Aged Women's Home at Markley Street and Coolidge Boulevard. The site was deemed the new location for the high school. In 1938, the school was opened. It was named the A.D. Eisenhower Senior High School. The school was named in honor of the principle that had served Norristown's high school for 43 years. In 1953, the Frank A. Logan Field was added. The school went through several additions and updates over the years. When the new high school in West Norriton opened in 1972, the school became a junior high.

St. Joseph's Protectory, Norristown, Pa.

Handcolored.

St. Joseph's Protectory for the Preservation and Training of Girls opened in 1888 for delinquent girls. The school occupied a building that was formerly used by the Oakland Female Institute. The school was staffed by religious personnel from the order of Our Lady of Charity of the Good Shepherd. The school closed in 1968 and was located between Sandy Hill Road and Main Street, bordered by Walnut Street.

Penn Square School, Eastern Norriton Township Montgomery County, Pa.

C. E. Schermerhorn & Watson K. Phillips. Associate Architects, Philadephia.

The original Penn Square school building was located on Germantown Pike below Swede Road. Norriton's school board built it in 1847. By 1896, the school had reached capacity, and a new Penn Square school was constructed. A six-room addition was added in 1929, but by 1936, plans for a new school were in the works. The school continued to grow and became an annex to the East Norriton Junior High School in 1973. In 1981, it closed as a public school because of declining enrollment. Today, it is the Penn Christian Academy.

Catholic secondary education began as a natural expansion of elementary schools on the parish level. After the organization of the Philadelphia Archdiocesan school system, responsibility for operating most parochial high schools passed into their hands. In 1955, St. Matthew's High and St. Patrick's High were turned over to the archdiocese. St. Patrick's was renamed Bishop Kenrick High School, and a new school was built on Johnson Highway and Arch Street in 1955. Architect George E. Yundt designed the school. In 1966, St. Matthews was renamed Archbishop Kennedy High School. Due to low enrollments in both schools, Archbishop Kennedy and Bishop Kenrick merged to form Kennedy-Kenrick Catholic High School in the 1990s.

In 1972, a new Norristown High School was under construction in West Norriton at the cost of $13.3 million. Classes in the new building started in the fall semester of 1973. The school is located on a 100-acre tract of property with entrances on both Whitehall Road and Burnside Avenue. The high school currently serves 1,600 students from the Borough of Norristown and East and West Norriton.

The first Lutheran Church in Norristown was Trinity Lutheran, organized in 1848. Under the direction of the Trinity Church, a mission was established in the West End of Norristown in 1885. This mission was Grace Lutheran Church. The church was built on George Street, north of Marshall Street, in 1886. In 1906, the congregation moved to a new church on Haws Avenue, north of Airy Street.

GRACE LUTHERAN CHURCH, NORRISTOWN, PA.
THE REV. JOHN W. DOBERSTEIN, PASTOR.

Norristown Pa.
MAY 19-12.
LAYING CORNER STONE   Reformed Church of the Ascension

Reformed Church of Ascension
Norristown, Pa.

The Reformed Church of the Ascension was organized in 1847, and its first church building was erected on Airy Street, adjacent to the courthouse. The church was rebuilt with a tower and steeple in 1859. The picture above is of the cornerstone of a new church being laid in 1912. In the late 1960s, the church was torn down to make way for expansion of the courthouse.

Norristown, Pa. St. Patrick's Catholic Church (Dedication)

The cornerstone for St. Patrick's Catholic Church was laid in 1836. Actually the congregation considers 1835 its founding because it was officially established about a year before the construction of the building. The present-day building is the third home of the catholic congregation. In 1875, St. Patrick's School was opened. The first school was in the basement of the old church on the corner of Lafayette and Cherry Streets. In 1895, St. Patrick's moved into a new school built on the former Slingluff property at the northeast corner of Chestnut and DeKalb Streets. St. Patrick's had its own high school from 1941 to about 1955 when the new Bishop Kenrick High School opened its doors. Over the years, the school has remolded, renovated, and updated to accommodate the catholic community in Norristown.

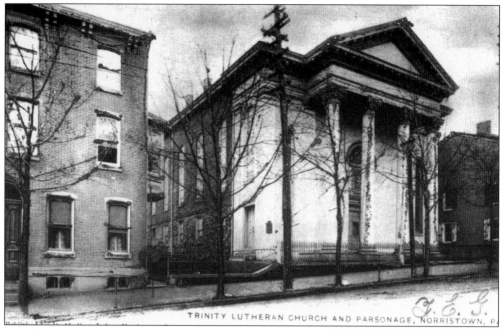

Trinity Lutheran Church and Parsonage, built *c.* 1863, reflects the Greek Revival style of architecture. At the turn of the 20th century, Louis Comfort Tiffany was commissioned for a major renovation, which included stained glass windows, alabaster, a bronze altar rail, and a glass mosaic. The church is located on DeKalb Street between Penn and Airy Streets.

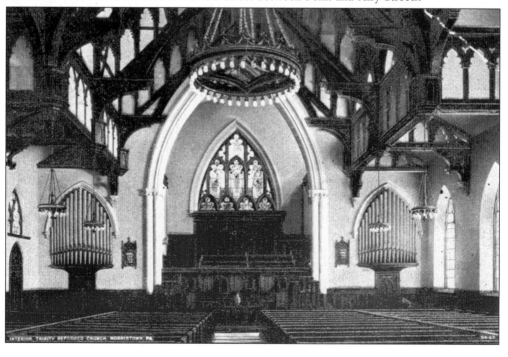

HAWS AVE. M. E. CHURCH, Norristown, Pa. (Home Camp-Meeting Decoration.) (Over)

In 1875, Rev. Michael D. Kurtz, pastor of Oak Street Church, arranged a meeting with members to plan a church in the West End of Norristown. A Sunday school was organized, and the first session was held in the Chain Street School. The cornerstone of the new chapel was laid in 1875 for the Haws Avenue Methodist Congregation at Haws Avenue and Marshall Street. The parsonage was erected in 1891. The cornerstone of the present-day church building was laid in 1896. A school was added in the 1950s. Andrew Carnegie contributed $1,300 toward a pipe organ for the church.

HAWS AVENUE M. E. CHURCH, SOUTH-WEST CORNER OF HAWS AVENUE AND MARSHALL STREET, NORRISTOWN, PA.

All Saints Church, Norristown, Pa.

All Saints Church was originally established as a mission of St. John's Episcopal Church to serve Norristown's West End congregation. In 1891, construction for the church began on Haws Avenue. The architect for the church was Charles Marquedent Burns of Philadelphia. Dedication of the church was held in 1892. On July 4, 1901, the church and parish house were struck by lightning and sustained severe damage.

BETHANY EVANGELICAL CHURCH

PUBL. BY I. H. BRENDLINGER CO.

6348   BETHANY ████████ CHURCH   NEW   NORRISTOWN PA.

Bethany Church had its beginnings in 1845, when minister Christian Myers met with a group of German speaking people meeting for religious services in the home of Mary Ann Schneider. The first church built by the congregation was on Cherry Street in 1867, and it was named Bethany Church. As the congregation grew it became necessary to build a new church. Ground was broken at Swede and Marshall Streets on March 18, 1907, and the new Bethany Church of the Evangelical Association was dedicated December 8, 1907. In 1968, Bethany was involved in a merger and became Bethany Methodist Church.

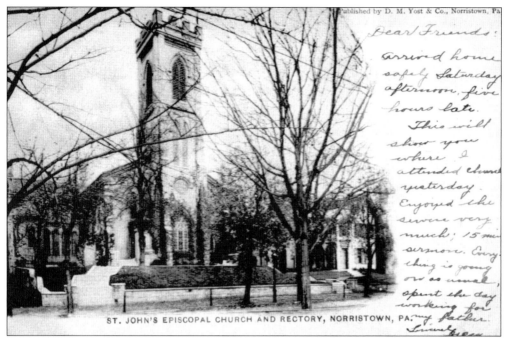

Published by D. M. Yost & Co., Norristown, Pa.

Dear Friends:
arrived home
safely Saturday
afternoon, five
hours late.
This will
show you
where I
attended church
yesterday.
Enjoyed the
service very
much; 15 min
sermon. Every-
thing is going
on as usual,
spent the day
working for
my father.
Sincerely,

ST. JOHN'S EPISCOPAL CHURCH AND RECTORY, NORRISTOWN, PA.

St. John's Episcopal Church was established in 1812, the same year that Norristown received its charter as a borough. The original church was built and consecrated in 1815. It was rebuilt in 1856 and renovated in 1898 due to a fire that ruined the interior. This wonderful Gothic-style church is located on Airy Street between Swede and DeKalb Streets. There is a churchyard at the rear where illustrious Norristonians and veterans of the American Revolution, War of 1812, Civil War, Spanish-American War, and later wars are buried.

FIRST BAPTIST CHURCH, NORRISTOWN, PA

The First Baptist Church, which began meeting at the courthouse in 1832, built its first church building at Swede and Airy Streets in 1833–1834. For many years, it was the only Norristown church that gave outspoken support to abolition and permitted abolition meetings in its building. It was also a stop and safe haven for slaves escaping the South via the Underground Railroad. The church building was rebuilt in 1873 but demolished in 1972. The congregation moved to a church in West Norriton. Today this is the site of One Montgomery Plaza.

125

First M. E. Church, Norristown, Pa.

219719

The First Methodist Episcopal Church was organized in 1832 with a group of 8 Methodist members. Within two years, the congregation had increased to over 100 members. Their first church building was erected on East Main Street below Arch Street. In 1858, the congregation moved to a new church building on DeKalb Street below Marshall Street.

Haws Avenue, Norristown, Pa.

The First Baptist Church fostered the organization of the Second Baptist Church at Haws Avenue and Marshall Streets in 1887. When its first building was completed in 1903, the name was changed to Calvary Baptist Church. First Baptist Church also established Olivet Church at Marshall and Violet Streets. In 1928, the Olivet congregation merged with Calvary Baptist.

The Rev. Joseph Barr organized the First Presbyterian Church congregation in 1819. They built their church at Airy and DeKalb Streets in 1854–1855. The tall spire of the church made it a town landmark, which can be seen from many miles away even today. The building is Italianate architecture with a Greek Revival facade. The church was also referred to as the "Brown Church" because of its exterior color at the time. Over the last century, the church has been enlarged several times and the interior repeatedly altered.

Siloam Baptist Church was organized in 1903, and the congregation held prayer services in a store on DeKalb Street. The growing congregation soon rented space and moved several times before purchasing property on Willow Street for their first church building. The church was erected *c.* 1908.

OLD CATHOLIC CHURCH, NORRISTOWN, PA.
PUBL. BY. I. H. BRENDLINGER CO.

This was the old St. Patrick's Catholic Church that was located on the corner of Lafayette and Cherry Streets. This church building was erected in 1836. The present-day building on DeKalb between Chestnut and Marshall Streets is the third home of the catholic congregation. In 1875, St. Patrick's School was opened in the basement of the old church.